D0985141

LOUIS
BRAILLE

DiscoverRoo
An Imprint of Pop!
popbooksonline.com

Emma Bassier

abdobooks.com

Published by Pop!, a division of ABDO, PO Box 398166, Minneapolis, Minnesota 55439. Copyright © 2020 by POP, LLC. International copyrights reserved in all countries. No part of this book may be reproduced in any form without written permission from the publisher. Pop!™ is a trademark and logo of POP, LLC.

Printed in the United States of America, North Mankato, Minnesota

052019
092019

 THIS BOOK CONTAINS RECYCLED MATERIALS

Cover Photo: Chronicle/Alamy
Interior Photos: Chronicle/Alamy, 1; Narinder Nanu/AFP/Getty Images, 5; Paul Seheult/Eye Ubiquitous/Alamy, 6; iStockphoto, 7, 8, 11 (awl), 13, 15, 17, 18–19, 21, 22 (right), 28, 30; Eye Ubiquitous/Newscom, 11 (background), 22 (left); Shutterstock Images, 12, 14, 20; marc zakian/Alamy, 23 (top); Frederic Cirou/PhotoAlto sas/Alamy, 23 (bottom), 31; akg-images/Newscom, 25; Monika Hlavacova/CTK/AP Images, 26; World History Archive/Newscom, 27; Collection PJ/Alamy, 29

Editor: Brienna Rossiter
Series Designer: Sarah Taplin
Library of Congress Control Number: 2018964784
Publisher's Cataloging-in-Publication Data

Names: Bassier, Emma, author.
Title: Louis Braille / by Emma Bassier.
Description: Minneapolis, Minnesota : Pop!, 2020 | Series: Amazing young people | Includes online resources and index.
Identifiers: ISBN 9781532163661 (lib. bdg.) | ISBN 9781644940396 (pbk.) | ISBN 9781532165108 (ebook)
Subjects: LCSH: Braille, Louis, 1809-1852--Juvenile literature. | Teachers of the blind--Biography--Juvenile literature. | Braille system--Juvenile literature. | Blind scholars--Biography--Juvenile literature.
Classification: DDC 686.282 [B]--dc23

WELCOME TO DiscoverRoo!

Pop open this book and you'll find QR codes loaded with information, so you can learn even more!

Scan this code* and others like it while you read, or visit the website below to make this book pop!

popbooksonline.com/louis-braille

*Scanning QR codes requires a web-enabled smart device with a QR code reader app and a camera.

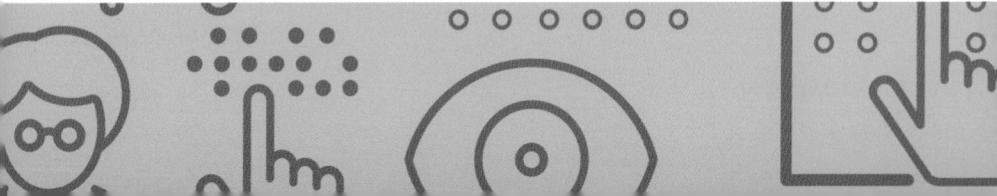

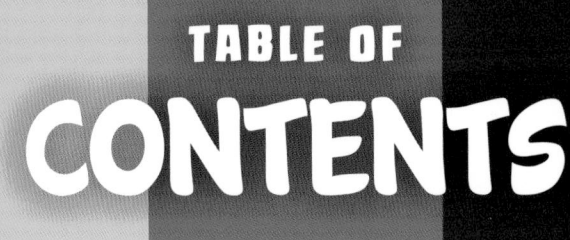
TABLE OF CONTENTS

CHAPTER 1
READING BY FEELING

Louis Braille lived in France during the early 1800s. He was a teacher. But he is best known for creating **braille**. People who are blind use this system to read and write.

WATCH A VIDEO HERE!

Louis Braille

Braille books use raised dots to represent letters and words.

5

Louis Braille grew up in this house in Coupvray, France.

Louis became blind as a young child.

At the time, few blind children went to

school. They couldn't read books or see

what the teacher wrote on the board.

Some blind students learned by listening.

But many never learned to read or write.

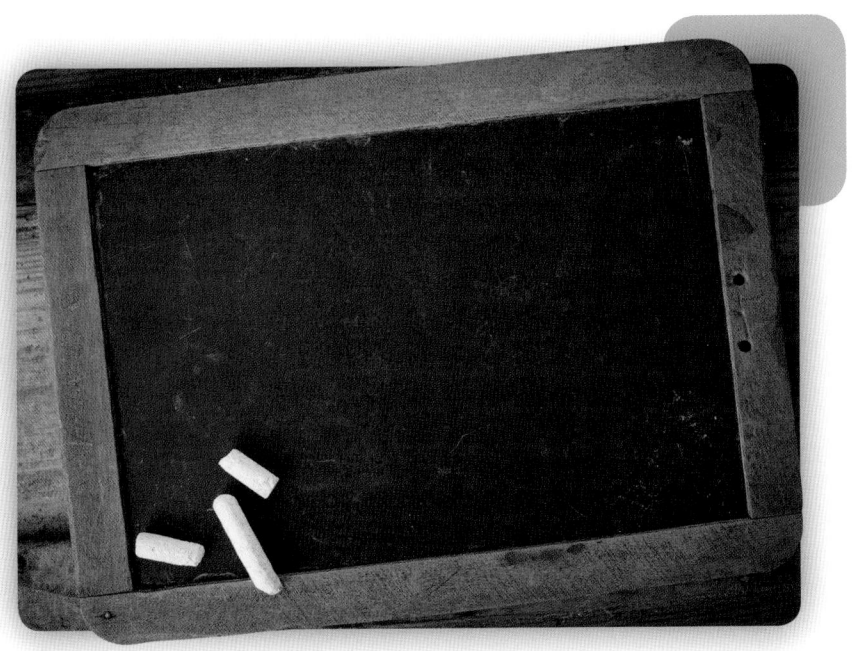

Long ago, students learned to write using a slate and piece of chalk.

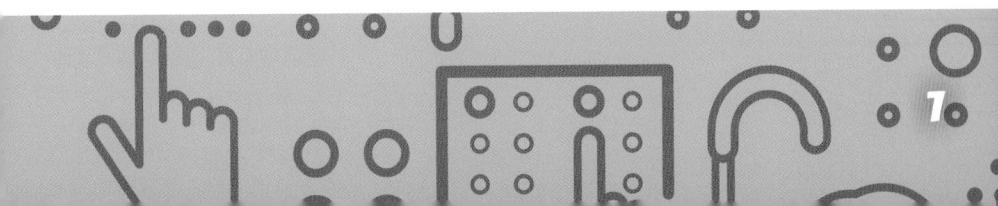

People read braille using their sense of touch.

Louis did learn to read and write. But systems for blind students were hard to use. Louis wanted to make them easier. So, he developed braille. This system uses raised dots. To read braille, people do not need to see the shapes of letters. Instead, they run their fingers over the bumps.

DID YOU KNOW?

Before braille, some blind students learned by feeling letters made from wood. Others felt letters pressed into wax tablets.

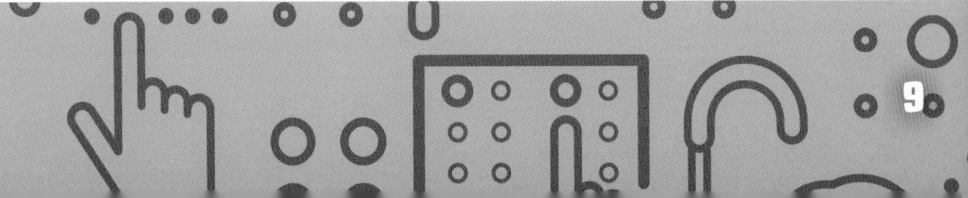

CHAPTER 2
EARLY LIFE

Louis Braille was born on January 4, 1809. He grew up in a small village near Paris, France. Louis often played in his father's workshop. When he was three years old, Louis had an accident. One of

LEARN MORE HERE!

Louis's father used many tools to shape leather.

the sharp tools in the workshop hurt his

eye. Both of his eyes became **infected**.

DID YOU KNOW? Louis's father made saddles and harnesses for horses.

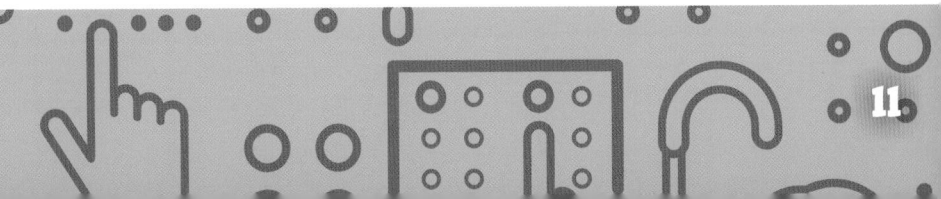

![National Institute for Blind Youth building illustration]

The National Institute for Blind Youth was the first school created especially for children who were blind.

By age five, Louis was completely

blind. At age ten, he began attending the

National **Institute** for Blind Youth.

This school taught blind children to read.

They used books with raised letters.

A statue of the school's founder, Valentin Haüy, stands outside it.

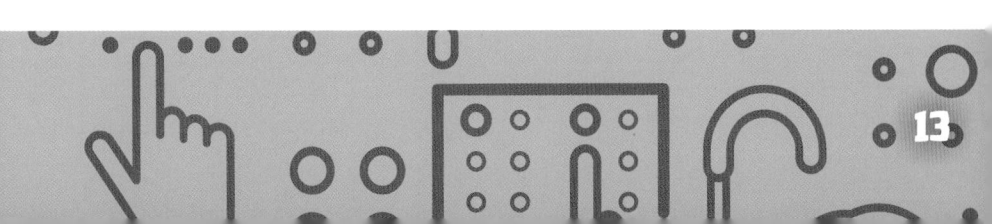

Charles Barbier was a captain in the French Army.

In 1821, Charles Barbier visited the

school. He taught the students a system

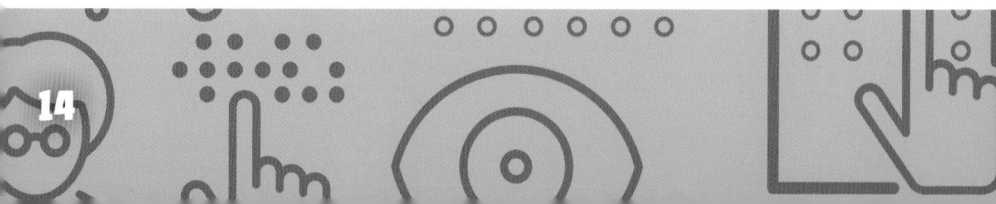

Barbier led soldiers during the Napoleonic Wars (1803–1815).

called sonography. This system used raised dots to represent sounds. The dots were arranged in groups of 12.

SONOGRAPHY

Sonography was also called night writing. Charles Barbier created it to help soldiers send messages silently at night. But his system was hard to learn. It used many different dot **combinations**. And the dots stood for sounds, not letters, so spelling and punctuation were difficult.

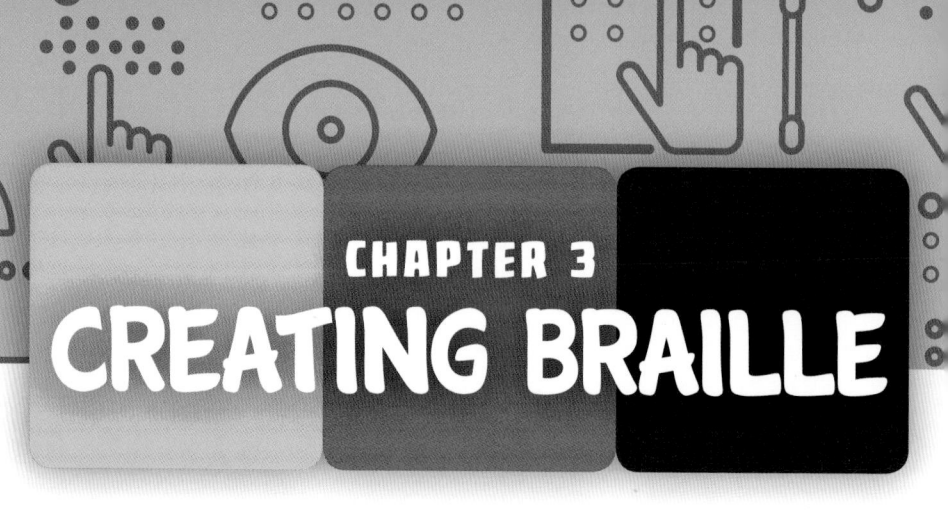

Louis thought he could improve Barbier's system. He made a **code** that used groups of six dots. A different **combination** of dots stood for each letter of the alphabet. Louis's system had fewer combinations than sonography. As a result, it was easier to learn.

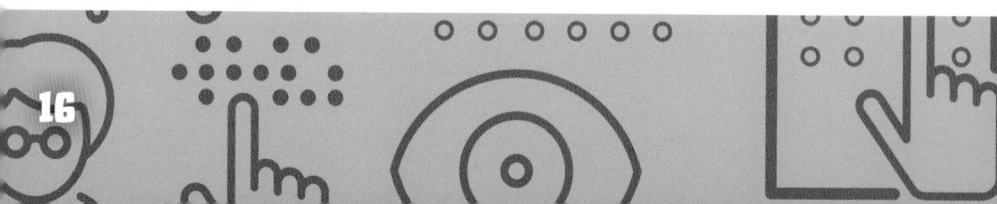

THE BRAILLE ALPHABET

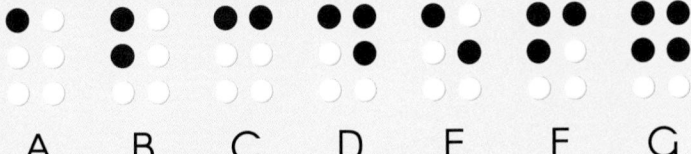

A B C D E F G

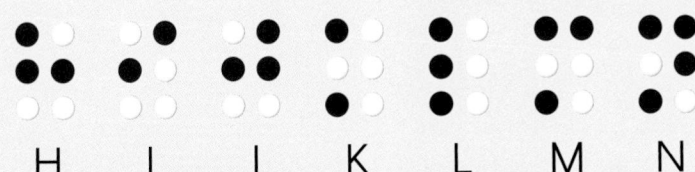

H I J K L M N

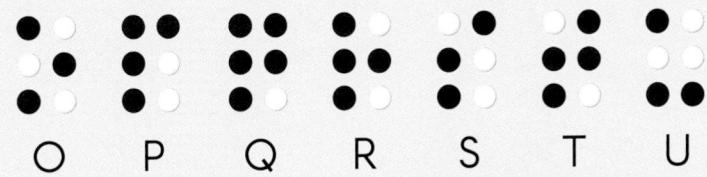

O P Q R S T U

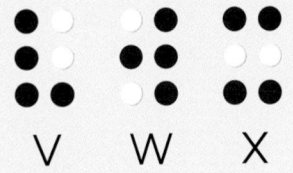

V W X

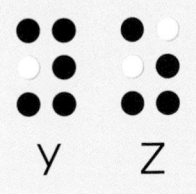

Y Z

COMPLETE AN ACTIVITY HERE!

● raised dots

Students used a **slate** and **stylus** to write **braille**. First, they placed the slate over a piece of paper. The slate's

18

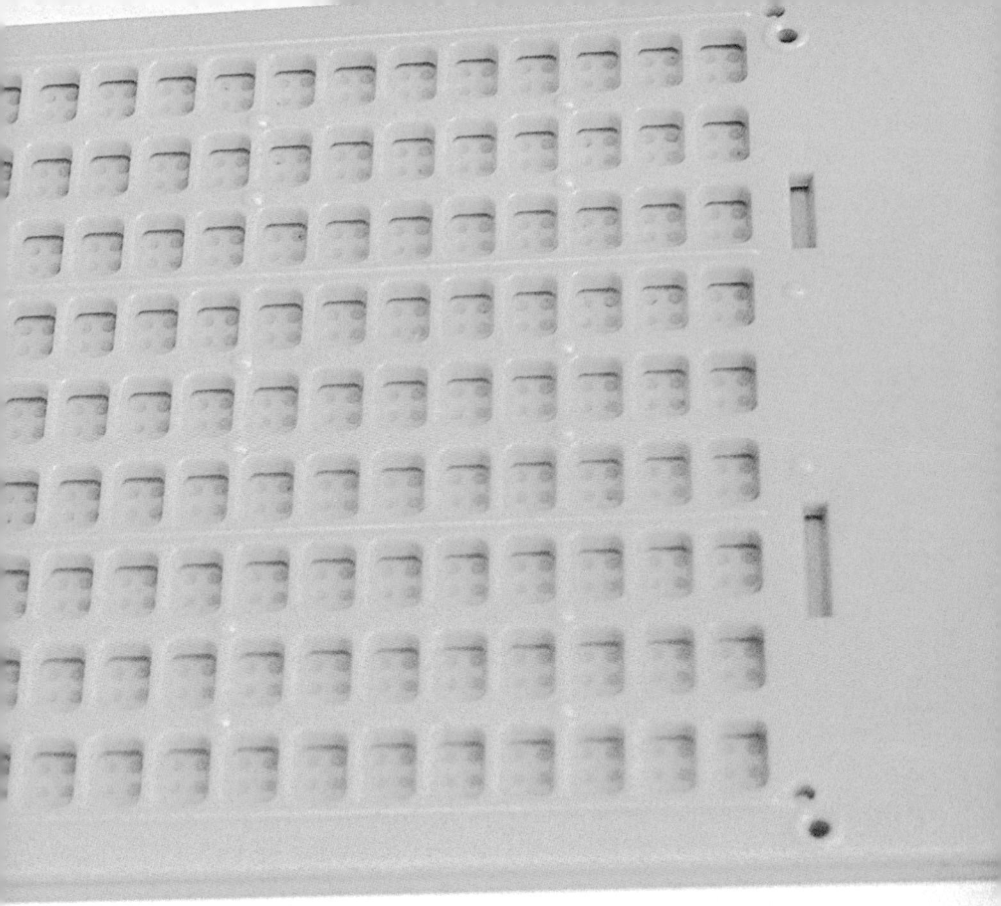

A person presses the stylus inside the slate to create bumps on the page.

many holes formed straight lines. Each

hole had a group of six dots.

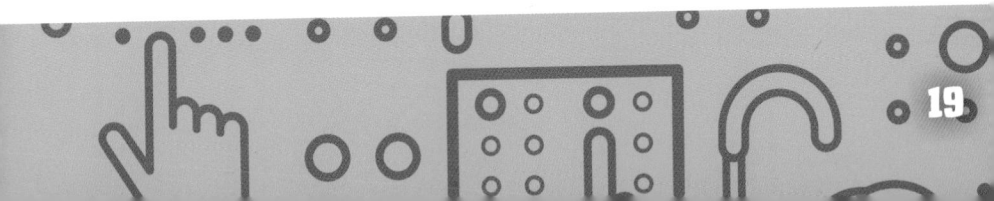

A person feels the page to read braille.

People used each hole to write one letter. They put the stylus in the hole. Then they pressed down. The stylus poked the paper. It created raised dots on the other side. When people turned

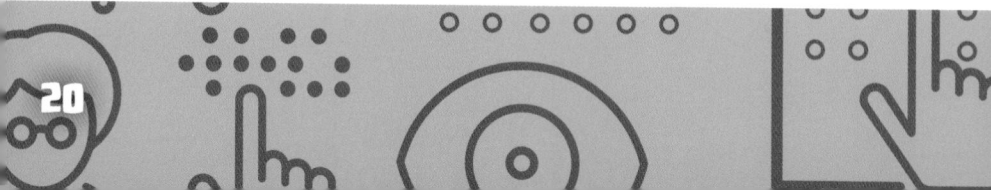

the paper over, they could feel the dots and read the writing.

DID YOU KNOW?

Later on, people created keyboards and typewriters that could write braille.

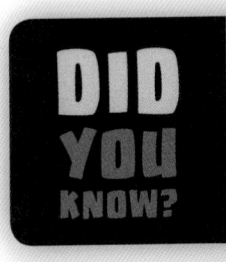

A braille typewriter creates bumps when users press keys.

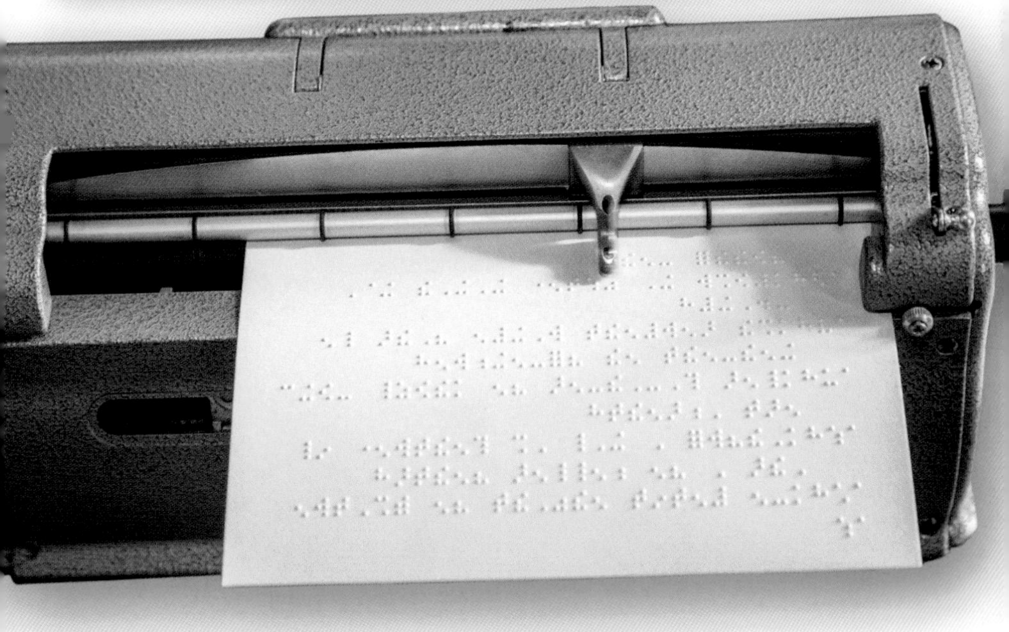

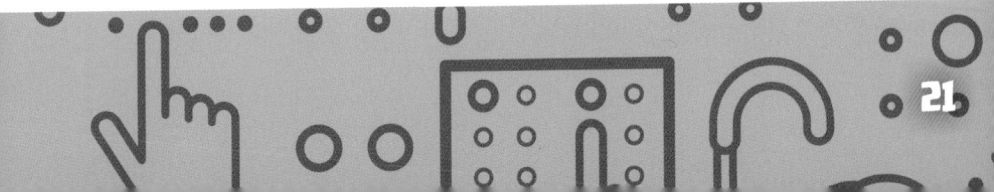

TIMELINE

1809
Louis Braille is born in Coupvray, France, on January 4.

1824
Louis invents a system of six raised dots. It becomes known as braille.

1819
Louis begins school at the National Institute for Blind Youth.

1852

Louis dies on January 6.

1829

Louis writes a book about braille.

1854

The National Institute for Blind Youth starts officially teaching braille to students.

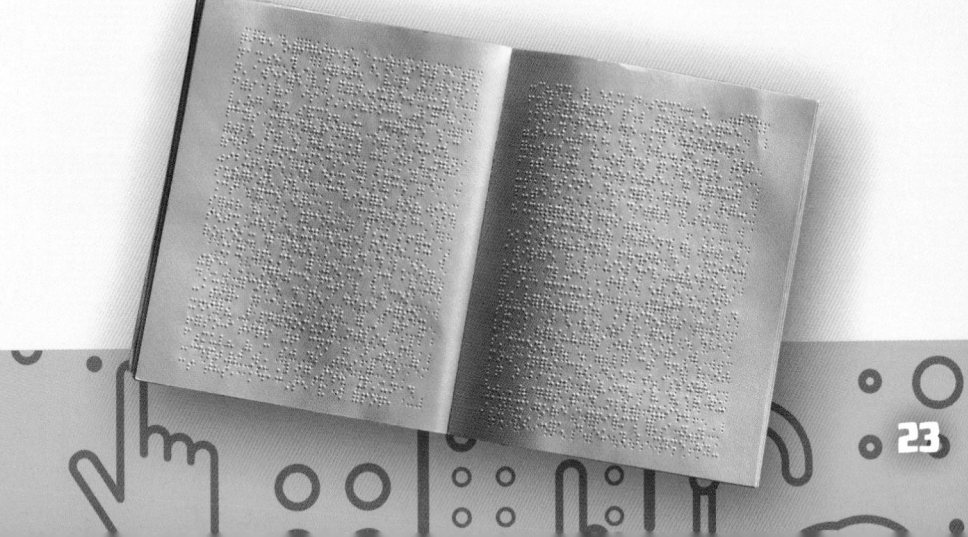

CHAPTER 4
LOUIS'S LEGACY

Louis began teaching classes at the **Institute** when he was 19. He taught history, music, and math. He also showed others how to read and write **braille**. Soon other students were using it.

LEARN MORE HERE!

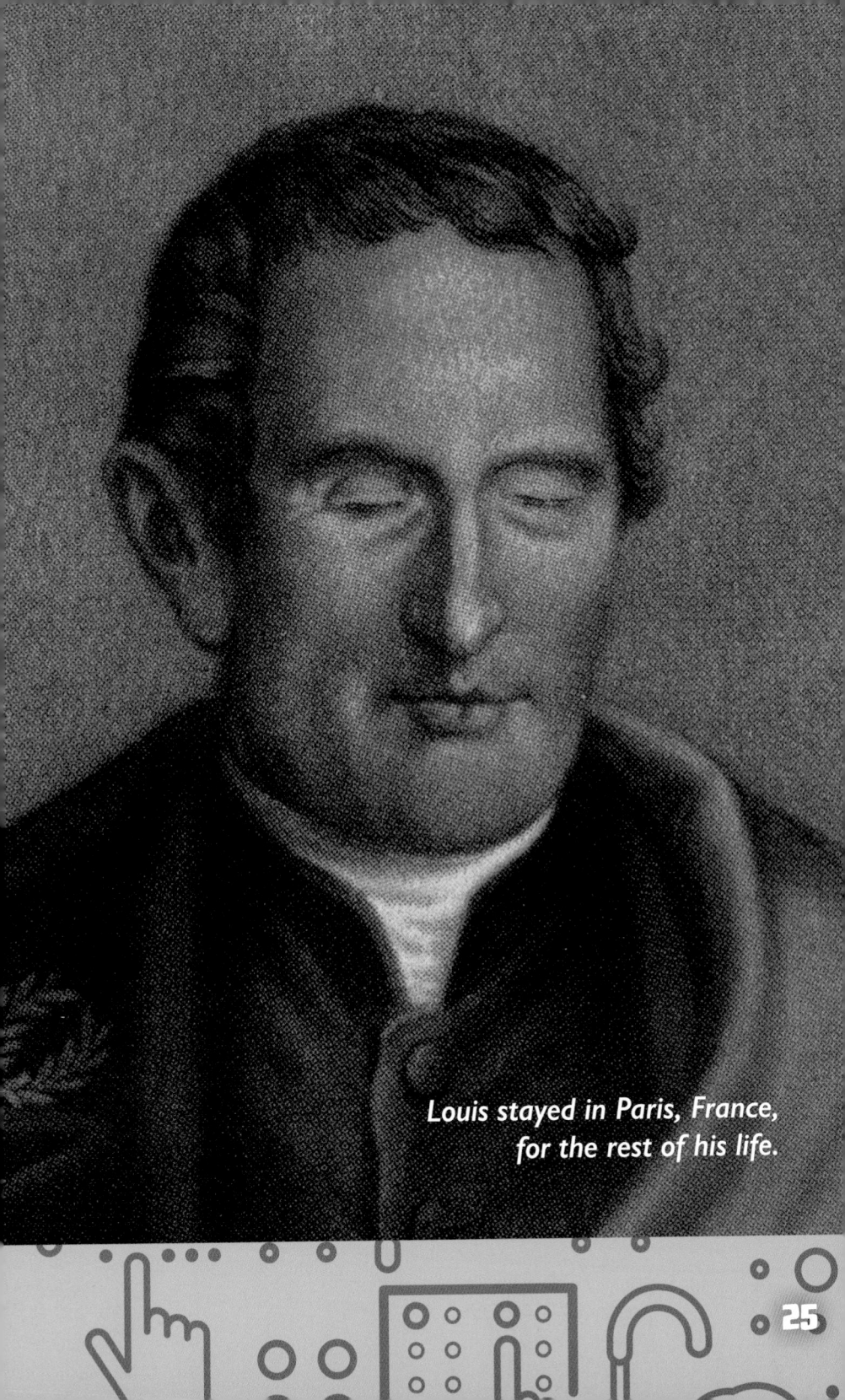

*Louis stayed in Paris, France,
for the rest of his life.*

Louis wrote a book about his system in 1829. He continued working to improve the system. By the time he died in 1852, braille had begun to spread. The Institute began officially teaching

In 1841, a student named Pierre Foucault invented a machine for typing braille.

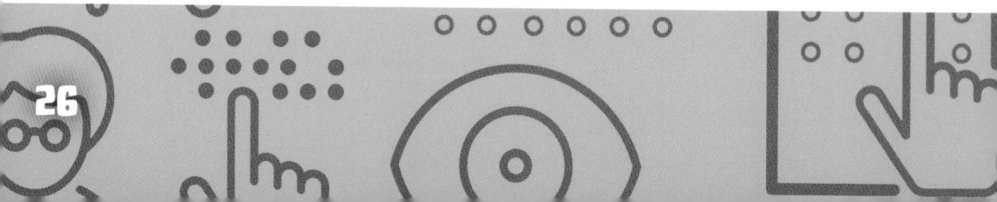

Students in Palestine study braille.

students braille in 1854. Braille became

common throughout France. Other

countries began using braille as well. And

new machines made braille books easier

to print and write.

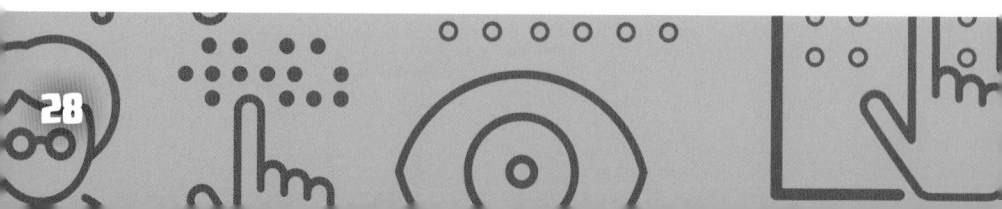

Braille often appears on buttons or signs.

Today, people all around the world

use braille. There are many versions.

A pianist reads braille music.

Some are

for different

languages.

Others are for

music or math

problems.

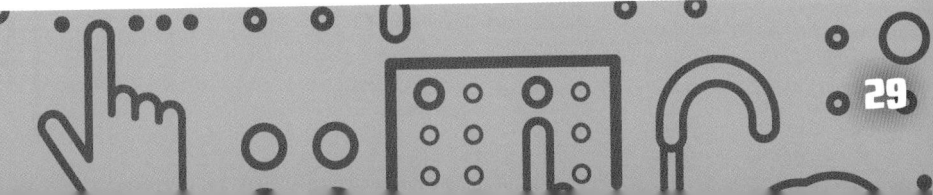

DID YOU KNOW? Louis played the piano and cello. He invented a way to write music in braille.

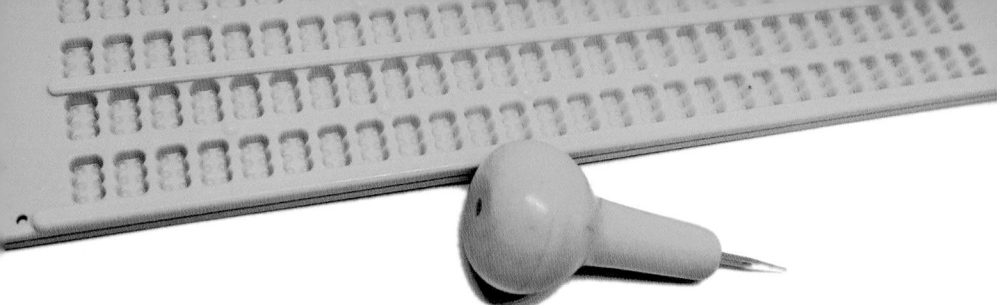

MAKING CONNECTIONS

TEXT-TO-SELF

Before attending the National Institute for Blind Youth, Louis learned by listening. Do you prefer reading books yourself or hearing them read aloud?

TEXT-TO-TEXT

Have you read a book about another inventor? What did that person create?

TEXT-TO-WORLD

Braille made it easier for blind people to read and write. What other inventions help make school accessible for all kinds of students?

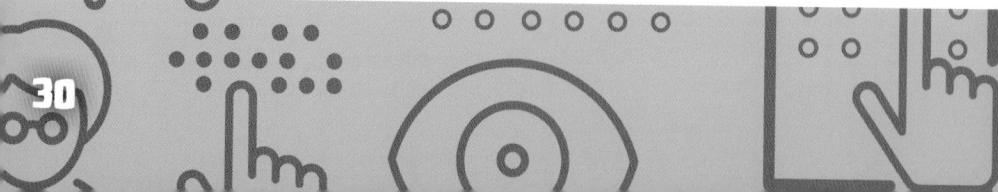

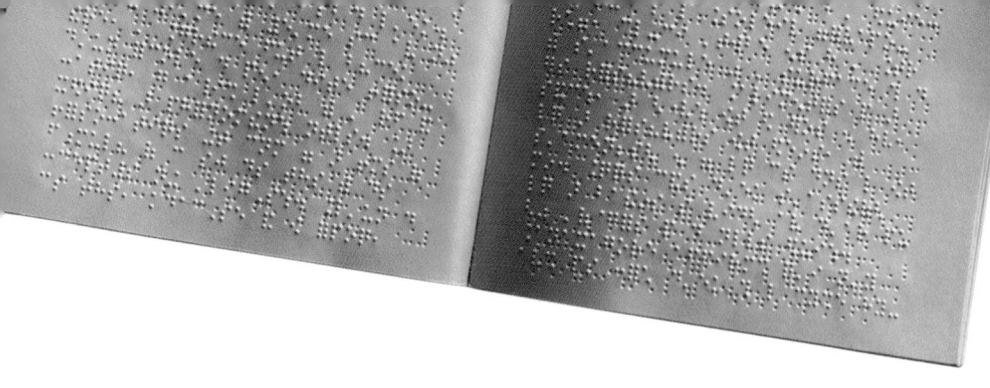

GLOSSARY

braille – a system that uses raised dots to represent letters and numbers.

code – a system of symbols, letters, or words used to write or communicate.

combination – a specific pattern or order.

infected – experiencing harm or disease as a result of germs entering the body.

institute – a school or group with a specific goal or purpose.

slate – a flat piece of metal or plastic with holes in it that is used as a guide when writing.

stylus – a small tool with a pointed end.

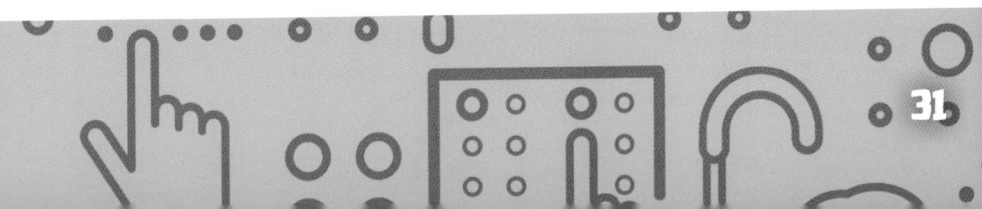

INDEX

ONLINE RESOURCES

popbooksonline.com

Scan this code* and others like it while you read, or visit the website below to make this book pop!

popbooksonline.com/louis-braille

*Scanning QR codes requires a web-enabled smart device with a QR code reader app and a camera.